Money Management

Published By Shaharm Publications

For a full list of books by Shaharm Publications, please go to:

http://www.shaharmpublications.com

Table of Contents

1. Why Manage Your Money?

As individuals, all of us have unique situations that need to be considered in life. Regardless of our circumstances, however, one factor which always needs to be considered is our finances. Regardless of whether you are just starting out and want to ensure that your finances are kept in order or if you find yourself in a financial bind and are not sure how to get out of it, the information available in this book can help. When you consider the benefits of managing your money properly, the need to do so becomes obvious.

One of the problems that many of us face is debt. Admittedly, most of us are going to have some degree of debt that needs to be dealt with, such as a mortgage or perhaps an automobile loan. Although there may be some adjustments that are possible in these debts, they are an expected and necessary part of life in most cases. Unfortunately, many individuals have found themselves in a tight situation where they are dealing with bad debt, high interest rates and a very tight budget. If you learn to manage your money properly, it is possible to overcome this difficulty and to begin to live a life that is free of those problems.

Retirement is also a concern for many people, and rightly so. Far too many individuals find themselves at retirement age without a plan in place. They may struggle for the remainder of their life and in some cases, are at the mercy of social programs that do not provide enough to cover a comfortable lifestyle. By starting early with the proper money management program, you can invest in your future and have enough money set aside to retire comfortably. In fact, there are ways for you to save enough money so that you can retire early, provided you are diligent in your efforts.

Even the best money management plan can be derailed, if there is an unexpected emergency. Regardless of whether it is a medical emergency or if it is one that is personal in nature, it can be devastating if you are not prepared. That is why one of the most important parts of having a budget is consistently setting aside money for savings. Although those savings may be available for long-term goals they can also be used for short-term emergencies, such as buying a new air-conditioning unit or an unexpected automobile repair, if you have a nest egg set aside. Having a small savings for this purpose can also help you to overcome those difficulties without using credit cards.

If you are raising children, it is likely that you have looked beyond their day-to-day needs to the future possibility that they may be attending college. A college education is an expensive prospect, regardless of whether they will be attending a university or a local, community college. There are programs available which can help you to save money for their college education, so that you can be prepared well in advance.

Finally, a benefit of managing money that should not be overlooked is an overall reduction in stress, compared to those who struggle with their finances. This peace of mind can benefit you in numerous ways, from your physical health to your mental well-being. Having your finances in order can also promote peace in the family, as most of the family arguments are typically about money.

By reviewing the information in this book, you will have an overall idea of how to establish a budget and to stick to it. You will find that establishing a budget is more than simply figuring out how much you spend on your bills every month. It is coming up with an overall plan that will allow you to pay your bills, reduce your debt and set aside money for savings consistently. So without further delay, let's get started on this journey in the next chapter, which will help you to establish your budget.

2. Creating Your Budget

Although there are many things that need to be considered when managing your personal finances, one of the first steps and most important features is generating a budget. This does not need to be difficult, but you do need to follow a few simple guidelines to allow you to generate a budget that will work well for you and your family.

It is not only important to create a budget for the benefit of your family; you also need to consider the ability of your family to stick to the budget. Realistic goals must be set and you need to be flexible when generating a budget, as well as any updates that need to be done over the course of time. Here is a 5-step process that will help you to create a budget that works for you.

Step 1: What Are Your Goals?

All of us have goals and these are things that need to be included in our personal budget. Before ever putting pen to paper, it is a good idea for you to identify your goals, both for the short term and for the long-term. For example, you may currently be saving to purchase an automobile or you might be trying to put a down payment on a home. These are short-term goals but they can help to shape your budget in a number of different ways. Long-term goals for your budgeting may include putting aside money for savings every month or perhaps establishing a retirement plan so that you can retire wealthy. When you outline your goals ahead of establishing your budget, you will find that it is much easier for you to decide which direction to go.

Step 2: Follow the Money

All of us have expenses and it is necessary for us to consider those expenses when generating a budget. In some cases, the amount of money that we are spending on specific items may vary from one month to another but in other cases, our expenses are fixed. Considering where you are spending money is an important part of generating a budget that is going to work for your family. You can come up with this information on your own but it is also a good idea to track your expenses for several months and adjust your budget accordingly.

Some of your expenses are going to be fixed and these will be paid every month, without fail. For example, you likely have to pay rent or mortgage, along with a phone bill, TV cable, an energy bill and other necessary expenses. Of course, it is possible to reduce many of these costs if necessary by living a frugal lifestyle, which we will discuss in a further chapter of this book. For the purpose of generating your initial budget, however, it is a good idea to stick with an average.

Many of the expenses that are put into the budget are going to be variable, such as the amount of money that you are spending on food or gas. Although you may have a general idea of how much money you spend on these items, it is something that can vary, depending upon your needs and how much you are willing to step outside of the boundaries of always eating at home or of avoiding driving needlessly.

Finally, you need to consider the extra expenses that may be included in your budget but are not necessarily a fixed way of living. For example, you may enjoy eating at restaurants or perhaps you want to go to the movies, which are certainly extra expenses but are not something that is necessary in order to live a frugal lifestyle. These nonessential expenses need to be considered, because they are an important part of life that help to keep us sane and relaxed so that we can enjoy the life that we are living. Of course, it is possible to reduce our nonessential expenses, but try to be realistic when generating your budget.

One other expense, which is often overlooked and is not generally included in the major expenses, is savings. Money should be set-aside on a monthly basis and it is far easier for you to save money if you include it as part of your regular budget. Having money set aside will allow you to pay for unexpected expenses without accruing additional debt. Otherwise, it will be available for something enjoyable at some point in the future.

Step 3: Where Is the Money Coming from?

Many households have a fixed amount of income every month that may come from a job, alimony or child support. There may also be those of us who are self-employed and, although we may make an average amount of money every month that can be spread over the course of the year, that amount may vary from one month to the next.

In this step of generating a budget, it is important to consider all of our income and to be as exacting as possible when putting it down on paper. This is also the step where math first enters into the budget, because you will be able to take your income and subtract your expenses to see if you have a surplus or at the very least, if you break even.

Step 4: Be Willing to Adjust

If your budget looks good at this point and you have some excess money available every month, you may want to live with the budget for a few months to see how it goes. If you find that you are able to stick to the budget and put savings aside every month, you have something that is workable and can be a basis for any future budget that is necessary.

On the other hand, there may be times when we find it difficult to stick to our budget, either because we underestimated the amount that we spend or overestimated the amount that we earn. In either case, it may still be possible for you to stick with a budget by adjusting the amount that you spend or increasing the amount that you earn.

In most households, a lot of time is spent earning money and, although you may be able to earn more, it is not always in the best interest of the family to do so. That is why it may be necessary for you to cut expenses in some way or another in order to stick to a budget. This can be done in a number of different ways. Perhaps you can simplify your lifestyle in some way, living in a smaller apartment or perhaps driving a less expensive automobile. You may also be able to adjust your budget in other ways by saving money on unnecessary expenses or by reducing your grocery bill by using coupons. These are a few subjects that will be discussed further in another chapter of this book.

Don't Be Afraid to Use a Tool

Although it is a good idea for you to write everything down on paper, there certainly are tools available which help to make budgeting much easier. Software programs, applications for your smartphone and templates that can be downloaded and printed will come in handy throughout the process. These can also help to speed up the process of generating a budget and make it more likely that you will avoid mistakes along the way.

Budgeting certainly is the most important part of managing your money and it is the first step in living a lifestyle that is debt-free and comfortable. In the next chapter, we are going to discuss some of the ways that you can live with your budget and do so comfortably.

3. Living With Your Budget

Although some of us may make excessive amounts of money that make it easy for us to stick to a budget, many of us are going to be rather tight when it comes to budgeting. Of course, we do need to factor in various unnecessary comforts and recreation, but there are also times that we're going to need to make adjustments so that we can live happily within our budget. Here are a number of ways that you can adjust your lifestyle so that you can live on a budget without feeling overly restricted.

Use the Available Tools - As we discussed in the previous chapter, it is important to set a budget and stick to it. A wide variety of tools are available to help you with this, but there are also tools that can help you to live within your financial means in other ways. For example, there are apps and software available which allow you to establish goals and keep track of how you are working in that regard. You will also find tools available that can allow you to save money through your budget and in cutting your expenses.

Set Priorities - All of us have certain priorities and at times, we may need to adjust those priorities in order to live on a budget. Perhaps we grew up in a household that had an excess of money and we learned to live with that excess comfortably. Just because you no longer have the excess available, however, does not mean that you need to live uncomfortably, provided you adjust your priorities. In some cases, setting your priorities is going to be a matter of adjusting the electronics that you own and use. Although it certainly is nice to have a large screen TV, the newest computer and the best smartphone, those are expenses that are often unnecessary. Adjusting your view of technology is one important step in adjusting your priorities. It will help you to make the transition from being a spender to being a saver.

Where Do You Live? - The amount that you spend on rent or mortgage every month is fixed, isn't it? Actually, adjusting this expense and reducing your living costs by reducing your rent or mortgage can take a significant amount of pain out of budgeting. Although it can be difficult to learn to live in smaller quarters, the payoff can be staggering. Imagine if you were able to save $750 on your monthly living expenses. That's similar to giving yourself a $10,000 annual raise! Of course, you don't want to cramp yourself beyond comfort, but many of us are able to live in smaller homes or apartments without too much difficulty.

The Expense of Food - There is no denying, it is enjoyable to eat a nice meal at a restaurant but that can certainly blow your budget for entertainment for the month. Rather than eating out throughout the month, you can save a considerable amount of money by learning to cook well at home. A large part of cooking is in the procurement of the ingredients and once you understand how to use coupons and shop in bulk, you can save a considerable amount of money. When you consider the fact that feeding a family of four with a delicious meal at home may cost $25 or less, compared to $75 or more at a restaurant, the benefits of eating at home become obvious.

Get Creative - As anyone who has been on a budget can tell you, there are times when you are going to get sick and tired of budgeting. This can be a real problem, because it can lead to binge spending and you may blow your budget in one episode, setting yourself back many months. When you find yourself getting completely tired of living on a budget, why not simply reward yourself by being creative? There are plenty of things that you can do which will give you some relief and allow you to bend the rules without completely breaking them. Looking for inexpensive meal deals in your local area or perhaps even taking a cheap vacation can rejuvenate you and allow you to get back on track again.

4. Short Term and Long Term Planning

One of the most important factors of money management is setting proper goals. This was discussed briefly in the chapter on establishing your budget, but in this chapter, we're going to expand on the idea and help you to see just how setting the proper goals and working toward them can help you in your overall management of money. More specifically, we're going to discuss both long-term and short-term planning and how they can help you in your quest for financial security.

Short-Term Goals

It is true that the majority of goals that you're going to set for your financial lifestyle are going to be short-term goals. Some of them may last for several years, but at some point or another, they may need to be adjusted. It is also important to understand that many long-term goals start out as short-term goals but they lend themselves to longer-term goals at some point in the future. Being able to establish short-term goals allows you to live on a month-to-month basis and to stick with the budget that has financial planning in mind.

Of course, it is important for you to establish any immediate goals that are necessary for proper budgeting as well. For example, if you establish a budget and you find that you are spending more money than you are making every month, you need to rectify that situation immediately. This can either be done by increasing the amount of money that you make or by reducing the amount that you are spending. In either case, there is no way for you to get around the necessity of forming an immediate goal and sticking to it.

It is also important to recognize that not all of our financial goals are going to be directly related to our finances. For example, you may be able to increase the amount that you save every month but you may only be able to do so by working excessive hours, which takes time away from the family. That is why it is important for you to establish both financial and personal goals and allow them to work in conjunction with each other for everyone that is involved.

Long-Term Goals

While short-term goals may be necessary for short-term benefits, long-term goals can motivate you buy dangling a carrot in front of your nose, so to speak. That doesn't mean, however, that you should be unrealistic when setting any long-term goals for the future.

An example of a long-term goal is establishing how and where you want to retire. Perhaps you currently live in a part of the world that is cold and, although you are able to make your living in that part of the world, that doesn't mean that you want to spend your golden years in the same area. If it is your goal to retire someplace warm and have plenty of money so that you can enjoy your retirement, it certainly can motivate you to work harder and to save money.

Not all of us are going to be able to have carte blanche when it comes to our long-term goals, however, so we need to keep them realistic. Although it can be motivating to imagine yourself living on a warm, white sand beach in a tropical part of the world, if you recognize the fact that it is unrealistic for you, it is unlikely that you are going to stick to your budget to reach the goal.

The Six P's of Goal Setting

Anytime you set a goal, it is necessary for you to follow an established set of rules that will allow you to achieve it. These are sometimes referred to as the six P's of goal setting.

Prioritize - In order for you to achieve the majority of your goals, you need to prioritize them. Reach for those that are attainable first and keep the others as motivation for working harder.

Positive - Negative thinking can make it difficult for you to achieve your goals. When writing out your goals or when thinking about them, use positive language, such as "I will" or "I have".

Precision - When setting goals, you need to be precise. This will help you to stay focused on the goal and to achieve it, rather than having a vague idea of what you would like to accomplish at some point in the future. Be precise about the specific goal and about the timing as well.

Performance - Establishing specific goals is important but from time to time, you need to measure your performance. For example, if your goal is to save $200 per month, do you have an additional $2400 in savings at the end of the year? If not, you need to consider your performance.

Practicality - Setting goals that are out of reach or impractical accomplish nothing. By setting goals that are within your reach, you will find it to be motivating because you are reaching them.

Personal - Finally, make sure that you are setting personal goals that are of interest to you. Although it helps to have feedback from others when you are setting goals, do not allow their opinion to overshadow your needs and desires.

5. Saving Money or Eliminating Debt?

It may seem like a simple decision as to whether you should pay off existing debt or save money when you are trying to determine your budget. After all, the amount of money that you can earn on savings is far less than what you may pay on the debt that you have accumulated. Things are not always as they appear, however, and there are some considerations for saving money that may be more important than paying off the debt that you have. Here is the information that you will need to make this decision on your own.

The Argument for Paying Debt First

Many financial advisors will recommend that you pay off your debt before you begin to save money. After all, as we discussed in the opening paragraph, the amount of money that you spend on interest for debt is much more than what you would be able to earn if you would set the money aside in savings.

Unfortunately, it can be difficult to pay debt if you are living in poverty and have no savings available. You may have a certain desire to see money accumulate in your savings account and, although you may still be paying interest charges on the debt that you have, it can give you a certain degree of security when you have savings set aside. This also makes it very difficult to pay debts, even though it may be in your best interest to do so.

It is also important to consider the availability of existing credit. If you have maxed out your credit cards, it is unlikely that you are going to be able to use them or to get additional credit, in case the need arises. Paying down your credit cards gives you that extra cushion and you can always purchase items on credit, if an emergency should happen to arise.

In the argument of paying debt before you save money, it is important to understand that having a certain cushion in your savings account is also necessary. Putting all of your money toward the paying of debt can end up backfiring on you in a number of ways, so it is more of a balancing act and in this scenario; it is leaning toward eliminating your debt as a priority.

The Argument for Saving Money First

Although you may be spending money on interest charges if you have accumulated debt, there are still many financial analysts who feel as if it is important for you to save money as a priority. This is especially important today, when the credit crisis has made the availability of credit difficult to forecast and having a nest egg set aside in case of an emergency may be your only hope for getting through a difficult financial time.

It is especially important for you to save money while continuing to pay your bills on a regular basis. Making the minimum payments may not make much of a dent in your overall debt, but it can keep you from accumulating additional debt if you are setting aside some savings. In addition, it can help to save your credit rating so that, when you do decide it is time to pay off your debt, you will not be as likely to lose the availability of credit. Many individuals find themselves in an unfortunate situation where they use all of their money to pay off a credit card or other loan and then have it closed on them because they are a "bad risk".

The decision to save money may be difficult if you are only looking at the situation logically. Spending money on interest is similar to throwing money away, but having a nest egg can give you peace of mind and it will be there, even if finances get difficult due to an increase in the recession. As you continue to save money and reach your financial goals, you can then begin to work on your debt by making additional payments, which will reduce it quickly.

Why Not Do Both?

Rather than deciding between paying off debt and saving money, it is possible for you to have a balance between the best of both worlds. If you are able to budget your money properly and have a significant amount left over at the end of the month, you can put some of it aside in a savings account and still make additional payments on your credit cards and other loans. Doing so will help you to enjoy both the benefits of reducing your debt and having a nest egg.

Another benefit of saving money and paying your debts at the same time is that it can help to retrain you to stick to your budget for the long term. Many of us got in the habit of overspending and under-earning before the credit crisis occurred and we may have extended our finances too far during that time. Seeing your savings accumulate and your debt reduce can help to give you the motivation to stick to your budget for the long term.

6. How to Cut Expenses

As we have discussed previously, there are two ways for you to adjust your budget. You can either earn additional money, which is difficult for most families or you can cut your expenses. In this chapter, we're going to discuss several different ways that you can cut your expenses at home in order to stick to your budget. Although some sacrifice may be necessary in order for you to cut these expenses, it is possible to do so and many families have found that they were able to cut corners without causing themselves too much frustration.

Dining in - When all things are said and done, one of the largest expenses for most families is the amount that they spend on food. In many cases, they may treat themselves to eating out several times per week and some of the meals that they eat in may be prepared at a restaurant and delivered to the house. This is an expense that can quickly eat into your budget and make it difficult for you to save any money. Eating at home is much less expensive and it can be enjoyable, if you make it a family affair. It is also much healthier, which can help to cut down on some of the unexpected medical bills that may come your way from time to time.

Reduce Your Housing Costs - Many families feel as if they must maintain extra space in their housing, regardless of whether they are renting or if they own their own home. One of the easiest ways for you to take a large chunk out of your budget is to reduce your housing costs. It is not out of the question to reduce your mortgage or rent by hundreds of dollars per month, provided you are willing to do so. If you are single or if you have extra room, you may also want to consider bringing in a roommate, which will also reduce your living expenses. Finally, consider some of the money that you are spending on furnishings in your home. If you regularly upgrade your appliances or furniture, this is an expense that can eat into your budget as well.

Take a Close Look at Your Electronics - Believe it or not, one of the largest expenses for many families comes in the form of electronics. Regardless of whether it is a large screen TV, a new computer or tablet or the latest smartphone, it is something that can get quite expensive. Although it is nice to have the latest gadget and it can work in your favor in many ways, it is not always necessary for you to be on the cutting edge. Look at the amount of money that you are spending on electronic gadgets and see if you can cut that expense. More than likely, you will find ways to meet your budget when you do so.

Reduce Your Utility Costs - It is possible to reduce your expenses when you are able to reduce your utility costs. Simply adjusting the temperature inside of your home by a few degrees or learning how to shut off the ceiling fan when you leave the room can make a difference in how much you are spending every month. This is something that is a cumulative and, if you are able to reduce your utilities across the board, you will find that it takes a chunk out of your budget as well.

Consider Your Transportation - Most of us love our cars and we would not typically think about making a change, especially downgrading. The fact of the matter is, however, this is an excellent way to reduce the amount that you are spending and it can take a chunk out of your budget. Lowering your expectations on transportation can help to save you money in numerous ways. Not only will it help you to save by reducing any auto loans that you are paying, it can also reduce your insurance bills. If you have access to public transportation, you may also want to consider taking advantage of it when possible.

Redefine Your Necessities - The basic needs for all humans include food, clothing and shelter. What we may consider to be a necessity for us and our family, however, may extend far beyond the basics. Of course, very few of us will be willing to reduce our necessities to the point where we are severely wanting. When you take a close look at your necessities in comparison with your luxuries, however, it is likely that you will find some ways to cut your expenses. Those expenses can be anything from TV cable to vacations, but all of them can be cut in some way or another if you're willing to do so.

7. How to Eliminate Debt

Most people carry some form of debt but it can quickly become a problem that will overwhelm you in numerous ways. Not only can it make it difficult for you to stick to a budget, it can cause you severe stress when the crunch begins to take hold. In order for you to get out from underneath debt, you need to take decisive action. Although it may seem difficult and it may take several years for you to completely see the realization of your goal, it is possible if you stick to a plan. Here are 6 steps that you can use to eliminate debt effectively.

Step 1: Where Are You? - Believe it or not, many people are not aware of where they are standing financially. They may recognize the fact that they are in debt and that they struggle from month-to-month to pay their bills, but they may not have a complete idea of how much debt is piled on top of them. It is important for you to figure this out from the start and make it part of your regular budget. Understanding where you are financially is important to determine how much is being paid monthly on debt as well as how much debt you are carrying. Do not be afraid to take this step, it will pay off in the long run.

Step 2: Stop the Bleeding - Now that you have an idea of how much debt you have, it's up to you to stop accumulating additional debt. If you have grown accustomed to using credit cards or any type of revolving line of credit, you need to stop doing so immediately. This is going to require that you carefully budget, so you should review the information in the chapter on budgeting. You must live within your means and, until the debt is gone, you may need to tighten your belt to the point where it hurts a little bit.

Step 3: Choose Your Plan - When choosing your plan for reducing your debt, you have a few different options that are available to you. Some people will want to pay off the debt that is attached to the highest interest rate first. Doing so is a good idea, because it reduces the amount that you are spending on interest by getting it out of the way so that you can focus on paying any other debt. Another option is to pay your bills with the largest balance first, regardless of how high the interest rate is on those bills. Doing so can be motivating, because it allows you to see some progress quickly but you are going to end up spending more on interest by doing it this way in most cases.

Step 4: Save - Although it may seem counterproductive, it is important for you to save money when you are reducing debt. Review the chapter in this book on savings versus paying off debt and you will see that a balanced approach is always best. Having some money set aside as a nest egg will prove to be beneficial if you experience any bumps along the way. It will also allow you to spend money on certain luxuries and unexpected emergencies without having to rely on credit cards or bank loans.

Step 5: Adjust the Terms - One of the struggles that many of us face when paying off debt are the high interest rates and unusually harsh terms associated with many credit cards. When you begin paying off your debt, it is a good idea for you to contact each of your creditors to see if they would be willing to adjust the terms. In some cases, they may significantly reduce the interest rate or can adjust the minimum amount due, which will allow you to focus on paying off other debts until you can begin paying theirs more aggressively.

Step 6: Get Help - Although it may be desirable to take care of paying off your debt on your own, there are times when help may be necessary. Credit counseling services are available which will help you to communicate with your creditors, come up with a plan and stay on target. Be sure you check the credentials of the credit counselors before you sign on the dotted line. There are legitimate companies available, but not all of them are going to have your best interest in mind.

8. How to save Money

Saving money may seem like a difficult task, especially if you're on a tight budget and are struggling to pay your bills. There are many benefits to saving money, however, that should be considered. Even if you are only able to put aside a little bit of money every month, it can accumulate over the course of time and can assist you if you have an emergency or even if you simply would like to treat your family to a short getaway. The process of saving money is fairly straightforward, but there are some things that you can do which will increase the likelihood that your savings will grow. Here are a few suggestions to help.

Be Determined - Before you do anything else with your budget, it is important for you to be determined in your efforts to save money. Make a plan that is reasonable and obtainable and stick to that plan consistently. Consider the fact that setting aside just $20 every week is going to end up saving you over $1000 by the end of the year. That money can really add up over time and eventually, it is likely that you will increase your savings if you stick to your budget.

Have a Goal - Although it is important to set aside money for long-term savings, you may also want to consider saving money for a short-term goal. For example, saving money for your family vacation or for a large purchase, such as an automobile, is easier done over a longer course of time. That is why it is important for you to continually save for these expenses and to include them in your budget. Rather than looking at them as unnecessary expenses, look at them as a necessary part of the budget that must be included, each and every month. In doing so, you will make it much easier to save the money and you will also be adjusting your view of savings.

Set Limits - If you are able to budget properly, you will have an excess of money every month. Some of this money is going to be allocated for savings but there may also be some extra money, which can find its way into your pocket. If you are able to reduce your extra spending by setting limits, you may be able to pop a little bit more into savings from time to time above and beyond what is in your budget. This can help you reach your goals much more quickly.

Save Your Return - If you are a low to moderate income family, you will likely qualify for an earned income credit on your federal tax return. This can be a significant amount of money, depending upon your personal circumstances. Make it your determination to set aside the lion's share of this extra money and distribute it among your long-term savings and short-term savings goals. It is also beneficial if you treat yourself during that time, so you don't feel as if you are restricting yourself beyond limits.

Work-Related Retirement Programs - One of the most important things that you can do for long-term savings is to take advantage of any work-related retirement program that your employer may offer. In many cases, they will match a portion of your contribution, provided it comes directly off of your paycheck. When saving for retirement, it is important to take advantage of this opportunity, because it can make a significant difference in how much money is being set aside.

Consider Investing - Although you should always follow the axiom, never invest more than what you are willing to lose, it may be of benefit to invest some of your money. Look for a local investment development account program in your local area, which will assist you in learning how to save money while in most cases, doubling the amount that you save in the account.

9. Protecting Your Family with Insurance

Throughout the course of this book, we have discussed the importance of getting on a budget, saving money and if possible, increasing your income. These are all important elements of your financial plan but one element that is often overlooked is insurance. Having the right type and amount of insurance can make a significant difference in your overall financial goals. It can help to protect you and your family in the event of a catastrophic problem, such as a disability, accident or death.

When deciding on what type and how much insurance is necessary, you need to consider your personal circumstances. In many cases, the amount of money that you spend on insurance depends upon your own personal situation in life, including your personal budget, your family situation and your age. There are a wide variety of policies available to assist you through a number of problems, should they happen to arise.

Although there is not a single policy that is going to work for everyone, there are enough choices available to suit any need. Here are some types of insurance that you would want to consider.

Auto Insurance - In every state in the United States, it is required that you purchase auto insurance if you own an automobile. This is often considered to be a fixed part of the budget, but there are ways for you to adjust this figure, depending upon the type and the amount of insurance that you have. It is important for you to properly estimate the amount of insurance that is necessary, because you would not want to come up short, in case of an accident.

Each state is going to set a minimum amount of insurance that is necessary in order for you to own an automobile. This would likely require liability insurance, but the state required minimum is often far less than what you would want to carry for your own personal needs. Additional types of insurance that may be available include fire, collision and theft, which should be considered on any vehicle of value.

Carrying extra insurance can help to protect you and your family, in case you run into a difficulty with an accident. There are ways for you to reduce the amount of money that you are spending on auto insurance, without reducing your coverage. One of the easiest ways for you to adjust your insurance costs is to raise the deductible. You can also shop around at different insurance companies, as there may be a difference in what they are charging. Finally, make sure that you are asking for any discounts which may be available through the insurance company, such as those that may be offered to safe drivers, students with good grades or non-smokers.

Health Insurance - You can pick up health insurance through your place of employment or privately, depending upon your situation. Having the right type of health insurance can assist your family to overcome a catastrophic issue with healthcare. Considering the high cost of healthcare today, this type of insurance should not be overlooked.

Disability Insurance - Along with healthcare insurance, disability insurance may help in certain circumstances. It can provide you with a percentage of your lost income, should you happen to become temporarily or permanently disabled. It is typically better if you purchase disability insurance at a younger age and look for a non-cancelable policy.

Liability Insurance - Carrying liability insurance can help to protect you and your family in case an issue occurs that uses all of your other types of insurance to the full. This type of policy is sometimes referred to as an umbrella policy.

Life Insurance - Although none of us want to consider the possibility of dying, we certainly would not want to leave our spouse or children without care, should the unthinkable happen. Having enough insurance to help cover the expenses of your family is more than simply providing them with burial insurance. You should look at your financial situation and consider how much is necessary in order for your family to live their life without having to significantly change it.

There are 2 basic types of life insurance. These differ significantly and you may want to talk about the differences with your insurance agent. Term life insurance is less expensive but it is only in effect for a shorter amount of time, which is the term of the insurance policy. Whole life or universal insurance is different, because it increases in value over the course of time and has a cash value, which can be borrowed against at some point in the future. It may also be possible to cash in the whole life insurance policy, if you surrender the policy to the insurance company.

Long-Term Care Insurance - Many people make the mistake of assuming that their health insurance policy is going to cover long-term care. Unfortunately, those that find themselves in this situation are often at the mercy of social programs that are put in place by the state. By purchasing long-term care insurance, you are guaranteeing that your long-term care would be covered, should you happen to need to go into an assisted living facility or a nursing home. There are a wide variety of long-term care insurance policies available to suit most needs.

10. Making Your Money Work for You

In this chapter, we are going to discuss a variety of ways that you can make your existing money work for you. In doing so, you will find that you are better able to stick to a budget, pay off your debt and save money. In fact, those are some of the primary ways that will be discussed for making your money work for you. They can help you to reach your financial goals and can establish your financial situation now and for the future. Here are a few ways for you to make the most of the money you have available.

Budget - Although it has been discussed numerous times throughout the pages of this book, your budget is the most important factor for making your money work for you. Without a proper budget, you are unlikely to stick to any type of plan and will continue to struggle month after month, just to pay your bills. Having a budget allows you to control your money so that you can achieve financial security. Do not overlook the necessity of establishing a budget and sticking with it consistently.

Save - Again, the need to save money is imperative in any type of budget. Putting money aside now can help you in the future, both for the short term and for the long-term. Admittedly, it can be difficult to save money when you are first starting out on a budget but it does not need to be impossible. By setting aside just a few dollars every week, you can begin to accumulate a savings, which will continue to grow over the course of time.

Reduce Debt - If you find yourself in a situation where you are struggling with debt, it is important to reduce it starting now. Start by taking care of just one of your debts, regardless of whether it is the one with the larger interest or if it is the largest debt you have accumulated. Information on reducing your debt is available in chapter 7 of this book. By reducing your debt and eliminating it, you will have additional money available in your budget to work with.

Improve Your Interest Rate - Although the interest rates that are available on savings and checking accounts are much lower than what they were at one time, there are some more attractive options available. Check with smaller banks in your local area or credit unions, as they tend to offer more options to their customers. You may also want to consider moving your money to an online bank account with a higher interest rate. Admittedly, it is not going to make a large difference in your savings, but every little bit helps.

Target Your Savings - A simple budget is going to require that you set aside money for savings every month. If you make it a bit more complex, however, you may find that you are able to save more and make it work for you in unique ways. One of the best ways for you to do this is to target the amount of money that you are saving for a variety of needs. Set up individual savings accounts for all of your goals in order to keep yourself on track. This will make you somewhat accountable to your goals and it makes it easier for you to see the benefits of what you're doing.

Talk to an Investment Planner - Rather than simply squirreling your money away in a savings account, you may be able to invest the money if you speak to an investment planner. This is especially beneficial to those who are at the point in their budget where they are saving significant amounts of money every month. It may be possible for you to earn additional money, if you have a private portfolio or put your money in an investment vehicle, such as savings bonds or stock options. It is important for you to consider both the potential benefits and the risks of doing so.

Focus on the Now - Even though it may be tempting to play the stock market or invest in other avenues that are somewhat risky, there is always a possibility that you could lose those savings as well. If you look at your current circumstances, you may find that there are opportunities available which can assist you in saving additional money and making your current savings work for you in a much better way. Those options may be anything from opening a CD to investing in an IRA or 401(k) program.

Although there may be some benefit to investing in the latest IPO and the possibility of getting rich quick, far too many individuals see their savings dry up and go away because of bad investments. Take advantage of what you have available by exploring the opportunities and you may find one that works well for you.

11. Money Management Apps

Many families that are trying to stay on a budget take advantage of the electronic options that are available to help them to do so. In today's world of mobile maps and free software programs, it is not difficult to find those options. Provided you apply them in your life properly, they can keep you on the road to budgeting your money in a way that will benefit you. Not only will they help you to pay your bills, they will allow you to track your finances and even to save money, if you are diligent in your efforts. Here are some of the ways in which apps can assist you through the process.

Track Your Spending - Even the best budget can get derailed if you are not familiar with where your money is going. Mobile applications can make it easy for you to track your money and can even give you a rundown on how you are spending it. You might be surprised with the percentages, once you get a true overview of where your money is being spent. Having such a tool is one of the best budget options that are available to you, and it can help you to keep on track with your budget goals.

Generating a Budget - Although we have discussed setting up a budget many times in this book, it is still an important factor in keeping yourself financially stable. Unfortunately, many of us struggle to set up a budget and to establish it in such a way that it provides us with a reasonable way to distribute our money every month. Fortunately, it is not necessary for you to do all the work longhand. There are plenty of mobile apps available which can get you started on the road to building and maintaining a budget. Included among the mobile apps are also some software programs available for your desktop computer and even templates, which can be downloaded and printed.

Budget Traveler - If you enjoy traveling or if you travel for work related needs, it is important for you to consider your budget when doing so. Being out of town can quickly become a major expense and can cause your budget to strain to the point of breaking. There are some applications available that will allow you to track your budget, even when you're on the road. Many of these mobile apps work with multiple currencies and they allow you to organize your bills, track your expenses and can even alert you if your budget is in danger.

Split Your Expenses - Although this is not specific to your budget, it is an important app to have available, if you regularly take part in a group activity where the expenses are divided. Typically, splitting the bill will mean that somebody is going to end up paying extra, but not if you have the right program available. There are plenty of free applications, which allow you to organize this activity and to split the expense so that each person pays according to what they owe.

Don't Forget Your Bills - An important part of sticking to a budget is making sure you pay your bills regularly. It can help to maintain a high credit score, avoid extra expenses because of late fees and can even keep you on track for additional savings. Although it is a good idea for you to track your bills manually throughout the month, you can also use a program to alert you to the need to pay the bill. In most cases, these programs will alert you a week or 10 days in advance of the bill due date.

All-In-One Programs - If you are not someone who enjoys switching from one application to another, there are some nice programs which allow you to track all of your expenses, remind you of your bills and even keep track of your savings in a single package. These all-in-one programs are convenient, but you do need to make sure that you are backing up your data regularly because a single problem with the program could take you back to square one.

12. Money Management FAQ

Q: Is a budget a good choice for me?

A: It doesn't matter who you are or what your situation is in life, a budget can benefit you. One of the most important factors for making sure that the benefits are fully realized is sticking to the budget as closely as possible. This would include staying on track with paying your bills, saving money and even determining if there is a way for you to invest your money so that you can increase your savings. Be as realistic as possible when establishing a budget so that you can stick to it and see it through to fruition.

Q: When should I start investing?

A: When you first establish your budget, you should consider the possibility for investing right away. Investing does not necessarily need to mean playing in the stock market or putting all of your money on the line. There are plenty of ways for you to invest your money for the future, such as in a life insurance policy, IRA or a 401(k) policy, which will carry very low risks.

Q: Should I save money or pay off debt?

A: As was discussed in chapter 5, there are benefits to doing both. Depending upon the financial professional that you listen to, they may recommend that you save money, pay down your additional debt or do a combination of both. As long as you are paying your debts, there are benefits to having a nest egg. It can help to keep you out of trouble financially if an emergency should arise and will help you to avoid using credit cards to pay for your immediate needs.

Q: What is disposable income?

A: If you make out your budget and you find that you have additional money left over at the end of the month after all of your bills, savings and additional payments are concerned, that is considered to be disposable income. It is always beneficial to have the availability of disposable income and you can use this money for additional savings or to pay on your existing debt to reduce it further.

Q: How will a budget affect my credit report?

A: Depending on your current circumstances, you should see an improvement in your credit report if you make out a budget and stick to it. Of course, the availability of a budget does not immediately reflect on your credit report but keeping current with your regular payments and reducing your debt can have an effect that is beneficial. In some cases, it may be necessary for you to get outside assistance to remove some of the negative marks against your credit, after you have brought them current.

Q: What is the benefit of a high credit score?

A: Having and maintaining a high credit score can benefit you in numerous ways. Not only can it help you to get additional financing in the future if necessary, it can also affect your ability to get a job and even to rent an apartment. If you have a difficulty with your credit report, you should seek professional advice to see how you can improve your credit score as soon as possible. There are programs available to help you to do so, and those financial counselors can also assist you in establishing your budget.

Q: Do I need to consider all of my debt when establishing a budget?

A: Although it may be tempting to cut corners and to adjust the numbers to make it look more pleasing to the eye, you need to be honest with yourself when establishing a budget. Make sure that you consider everything involved, from the amount of money that you make to the amount of debt that you have available. Even if you have stopped paying on some of the debt, it is important to consider it so that you can care for it and get the negative mark off of your credit score.

13. Money Management - Pass It on

Understanding the proper use of money management can assist us throughout our lifetime. It can help us to stay on track with our bills, keep us from accumulating unnecessary debt and can allow us to retire comfortably. Unfortunately, many of us were not provided with the knowledge about money management in advance from our parents. Perhaps they also struggled with finances or it may have been considered a taboo subject by your family. In either case, it is important for you to break the trend and to teach your children proper money management, so that they may benefit by it for the long-term as well.

One of the difficulties that many people face is knowing when they should start discussing money with their children. This has led to many problems, including having the children not fully comprehend where money comes from and how much they are able to spend. From the time that you are able to speak to the child, it is important to begin teaching them about money management. In that way, they will have an understanding that you earn the money by going to work and it is not simply something that you pull out of the ATM machine, anytime you need some cash in your pocket.

One of the benefits that are available from teaching your child about finances is the fact that they may begin to conserve money naturally. Although children will always enjoy spending money on anything from candy bars to toys, it has been shown that those who understand finances are more apt to save money and to be realistic in how they do spend it.

Providing your child with an allowance from an early age and making them earn the allowance is one of the options that is available which can be beneficial. It helps to teach your child about money and allows them to be financially aware. Doing this at a younger age is often beneficial, because young children are more apt to take your advice than teenagers.

The benefits of teaching your child how to manage money properly are seen at a young age but they also follow through later in life. Children who understand how to manage money and who come from a family that manages money well will be more likely to avoid financial problems in the future. It is something that you can pass along to your children that will have lasting repercussions.

In Summary

You can see from all the information in this book, that actively managing your money can be very good for you. Better-managed money leads to less stress, more opportunities to grow your wealth and do the things you want to, often better health, and generally happier families, as stress is removed.

Review the chapters again, choose some tools to help you and get started now!

www.ingramcontent.com/pod-product-compliance
Lightning Source LLC
Chambersburg PA
CBHW072312200526

45168CB00014B/1372